My Conquest of Mexico

Atlas of Mexican Conflict, Rand McNally and Company. 1913

My Conquest of Mexico

By Benjamin Muse

Parnassus Book Service

(C) Ben Muse 1973

First Published in 1973 by Parnassus Imprints

Second Edition 2018
ISBN: 978-1-7327626-0-2

Produced and printed in United States of America
by Parnassus Book Service, Yarmouthport, Mass.

My Conquest of Mexico

Until the adventure that I am about to relate, I had been a tolerably well-behaved North Carolina boy. It is true there had been one deviation from correct behavior sufficiently serious to be mentioned. At age nine I led two younger children, a brother and a cousin, one afternoon on a runaway, which gave our families something of a fright. We trudged to the edge of my hometown of Durham and about a mile into a forest. There were actually five of us when we left home, but two, who were neighbors, lost heart before we got to the woods and turned back. The three of us, tasting the joys both of adventure and of mischief, pressed on. We continued until night began to fall. Then we made for an opening in the forest and on to a road, which was indeed a welcome sight. In a few minutes one of those primitive early automobiles came chugging along, and it stopped for us. The driver was a stranger but he knew our parents and he carried us home on the back seat of his open car. (It was the first time we had ever been this close to one of those miraculous vehicles.) In punishment for this crime, I was confined to my bedroom for two days and my cousin Bill Shaw was forbidden to harness up his billy goat for two weeks.

During the next six years my conduct might almost have been called exemplary. I did very well in school, I read more books than the average boy of my age (I had a particular weakness for G. A. Henty and Sir Walter Scott), and I found time to earn considerable money. I made the money delivering newspapers and later writing school news and other small stuff for the Durham Sun. I went on an ice cream-eating binge now and then, but most of my earnings were deposited regularly in a savings account.

Beginning in about my twelfth year I became a voracious reader of newspapers. I also read Harper's Weekly, to which my family subscribed. I followed Teddy Roosevelt's break with William Howard Taft, the launching of the Bull Moose

Party, and the rise of Woodrow Wilson. But my real obsession was the Mexican Revolution. In those days there was little armed conflict elsewhere to compete for the world's attention, so the Mexican Revolution seemed tremendous. Mexico's heroes and villains, its battles and assassinations, and the rise and fall of Mexican governments furnished interminable copy for the American press and fascinated the public, especially me.

It started when the gentle idealist Francisco Madero led a revolt which ended in 1911 the 30-year reign of the Mexican dictator Porfirio Diaz. Madero ruled for 20 months amid mounting confusion. Then he was assassinated along with his vice-president, and the reactionary General Victoriano Huerta seized power. That set off a bigger and bloodier rebellion against Huerta. Older readers will remember all this. As more and more battles were reported in the press, the names of revolutionary leaders like Venustiano Carranza, Francisco Villa, Alvaro Obregon and Emiliano Zapata became household words in the United States. The swash-buckling "Pancho" Villa, riding to victory after victory over Huerta's armies (Villa's murderous propensities were little publicized at the time), was a popular favorite. Carranza was striving to unite the anti-Huerta elements, who were called the "Constitucionalistas", and had assumed the title of Primer Jefe, or First Chief. To most Americans these were the good guys, Huerta was emphatically the bad guy. That was in fact the view of the United States government. In April, 1914, American forces seized the port of Vera Cruz to stop arms from reaching Huerta.

In that same month of April, 1914, in peaceful North Carolina, I passed my sixteenth birthday. It was about this time that I ceased to be a sensible and reliable boy. I decided to go to Mexico. I began furiously to study Spanish and make other preparations for a trip to that land of drama and romance. By this time I was little interested in graduation from high school although I accomplished that with ease at the end of May. What was happening to me was not unlike the emergence of a butterfly from its cocoon. I withdrew from the bank my hard-earned savings, amounting to about $400—it was the first time I had withdrawn anything from that account and bought an elegant suitcase, a portable typewriter and a dashing new suit of clothes (a black-and-white check thing which I remember well). My role in Mexico would be that of a war correspondent. The bemused editors of the Durham Sun agreed to publish my "dispatches". (As it turned out, I would send them just one report, an uninspired account of Carranza's entry into Mexico City, which was indeed published.) I obtained a passport, which identified me as a representative of the press, and I bought a railway ticket to Monterrey, Mexico, where by the latest reports, Carranza's provisional government had established its headquarters.

What did my father say about all this'? My mother having long since passed away, Papa was both father and mother to me. In this, as in other crises in my life, he understood me better than anyone else. While others were discounting my talk about going to Mexico and saying: "He'll get over it"—Papa took me seriously and did not try to deter me. "I trust you to be a good boy," he said. "Only promise me that you will come back and enter college in the fall." He saw me off at the Union Station at four o'clock in the morning, reminding me that above all things I must come back in the fall.

At Charlotte, North Carolina. I had a few hours to wait before taking a Pullman for the rest of the journey. I called on the editor of the Charlotte Observer and that incredulous gentleman agreed jovially to publish some of my dispatches from Mexico. (Nothing ever came of that.) Going through Texas the next morning, I purchased a Mexican newspaper and got to work translating with the aid of my Spanish-English dictionary. At San Antonio a number of Mexicans boarded our train. I soon got into conversation with some of them who were kind enough to listen to my outrageous Spanish. I have always found that the quickest way to learn a foreign language is to abandon all reticence and talk, talk, talk regardless of one's mistakes. I followed that rule throughout my visit to Mexico, and, if indeed my Spanish remained faulty, I got acquainted with people wherever I went. I developed a friendship on the train with a young Mexican who was later to render me a great service. Although we got to know each other pretty well, I have been unable to pull his name out of the recesses of my memory, so in this one instance I shall invent a name and call him "Ruiz". He was returning to the headquarters in Monterrey from some errand in Texas.

I should emphasize the fact that I am writing

about things that happened 60 years ago. Fictionally, a great deal would need be filled in to make a good story, but I intend to relate only what I remember. And my memory plays some strange tricks. For instance my entry into Mexico at Nuevo Laredo remains almost a blank to me, although I know that I had no trouble with border officials.

The next thing that I remember clearly after the train journey through Texas was a visit to the American consul in Monterrey. The latter was an elderly, weather-beaten veteran of service in Mexico who did not seem to be at all busy. He found something extremely amusing about a 16 year-old boy playing at being a war correspondent, but I was very much in earnest and he gave me a formidable looking document with a red seal requesting courtesies for me as a representative of the American press. He also gave me an elementary run-down on what was going on in Mexico. I had gained a smattering of this from my newspaper reading. The revolution had reached a climax. The federal forces had been pushed back almost all the way to Mexico City, and President Huerta had abdicated. Yet the picture was not entirely bright for Carranza, the consul said. The First Chief was having trouble with General Villa, and he had no contact with General Zapata, who had conducted his own revolution in southern Mexico. Carranza had not been in Monterrey lately. His headquarters for the time being was in Saltillo, 50 miles away. Saltillo is the capital of the State of Coahuila, of which Carranza was governor.

The group in Monterrey were mainly civilian personnel concerned with problems of finance and administration and preparing to man ministries and bureaus when Carranza should take over in Mexico City. I did not know what I would ask if I should have an interview with any of these people, but I looked up Ruiz and he was glad to see me. I also met several other provisional bureaucrats of whom I remember only Ruiz's immediate superior, whose name was Flores and whose title was "sub-treasurer." One very busy official who was pointed out to me was Alberto Pani. I do not believe I actually met Señor Pani at this time, but I mention him because he was to be an important figure in Mexican politics for a decade and more. In later years in the American diplomatic service I would meet him as minister of foreign affairs and again as Mexican Minister in Paris. At this stage he was "general treasurer" of the Constitucionalistas organization.

My five or six days in Monterrey were uneventful and, perhaps for that reason, they are only dimly remembered. After the initial thrill of being in Mexico I was not entirely happy. I did not know just how to take hold of the business of being a war correspondent, and I wondered if I had come to the right place for great events. There were no other American newspapermen around; they had moved closer to the battle scenes in the south. I spent much of my time wandering about the city. Ruiz sometimes joined me at lunch or dinner. We observed a certain gaiety on the streets and in the cantinas over the news that the revolution was winning. There was some singing and a great deal of something like music coming out of gramaphones. One song could be heard endlessly and everywhere—La Cucaracha."

That famous song had many verses and new ones were composed almost daily. They were largely in ribald ridicule of the Hueristas, but the basic verse went:

La cucaracha, la cucaracha
Ya no puede caminar,
Porque le falta, porque no tiene
Marihuana que fumar

I had no idea what marihuana was at the time, but in view of the agitation today, it is interesting to note that this doggeral meant in English:
*The cockroach, the cockroach
Can't walk any more,
Because he's out of, because he hasn't got
Marihuana to smoke.*

My most strenuous undertaking in Monterrey had nothing to do with the Mexican revolution. It concerned the mountain that dominates the valley in which Monterrey lies. I resolved to climb that mountain. Viewed from my hotel window, Saddle Mountain seemed to rise from the very edge of the city. But I found otherwise: after four hours of hiking along dusty roads and through scrubby underbrush, I had not reached even its lower slopes. I was also getting farther and farther away from any place to eat. Turning around, I trudged all the way back, with no refreshment other than a

View of Bishops Palace and Saddle Mountain near Monterrey. Painting by Conrad Chapman, 1865

bottled apple drink purchased from a roadside vendor.

One day Ruiz said to me: "We are leaving for Mexico City tomorrow, and you are to come with us." Flores later confirmed the invitation. The bureaucracy cadre was moving south to join the military in the grand finale of the revolution and I was going with it! That trip was to be the miracle and the glory of my adventure in Mexico. How I, an American boy, came to be invited to go along I have never quite fathomed. There was no other American and no other reporter (if I could be called one) with us. I can only conclude that I was a harmless curiosity whom these Mexican politicians found amusing and who offered a slight relief from the tedium of what would be a long and, under the existing conditions, slow trek to the National capital. At any rate, there I was, traveling with a party of revolutionary big-wigs headed for the triumphal entry into Mexico City. From a practical point of view it was a rare stroke of luck. I had a no-expense VIP tour with my meals and lodging taken care of by the revolution. Except in the purchase of a few newspapers and postcards, I did not spend a centavo on the whole trip.

A fatal accident stopped our train about an hour out of Monterrey. It set us back one day, but in a time when tragedy and bloodshed were commonplace in Mexico not much was made of it. It was customary then to send a buffer locomotive ahead of any important train as a precaution against miscalculations or foul play along the way. Our buffer collided with a train carrying a handful of soldiers as it came out of a tunnel. We spent some hours at the scene and returned to Monterrey after nightfall, carrying an injured fireman and a dead engineer. The next afternoon we set out again. We suffered no other serious mishap on our long journey south, although we were delayed several times by cattle on the tracks. In one instance our buffer locomotive cut an unhappy cow in half and we stopped while men from the car that carried our little detachment of soldiers brought pieces of the severed animal aboard.

We lunched at nondescript villages where eating places and food had been prepared not far from the railway tracks, and local dignitaries turned out to greet our party. We dined and spent one night each in hotels in Saltillo and San Luis Potosi. In Queretaro our accommodations were arranged by the jefe politico, or mayor, in some kind of

Constitutionalist troop train, circa 1914

institution, but they were quite comfortable. (I visited the scene of the execution of the Emperor Maximillian in that city.) The important people in our party had business in each of these cities, conferring with local leaders and receiving and sending messages. I stayed out of the way and did a little sightseeing.

I had no feeling of being a nuisance on this train journey. Some of the more dignified people paid no attention to me, but they did not seem to resent my presence. A notable with whom I had a few words was Ignacio Villareal, who later held a cabinet office in Mexico City. My memory is again exasperating here: I have no recollection of Ruiz on the train; he must have left it at one of the stops and I never saw him again.

My regular companion on the train, and unforgettable, was Hector Bourges, a dapper Mexican of French extraction with a small black moustache. His card read "Jefe de Bienes y Confiscaciones," and his specialty was arranging for the confiscation of property required by the revolution. We shared a seat and chatted a great deal, exchanging my imperfect Spanish for his imperfect English. He had a sense of humor. There was a certain twinkle in his eye when he talked about his role as chief confiscator. Later in Mexico City Senor Bourges took me with him on one of his confiscation errands. This was to a elegant mansion which, he told me, had once been the home of Pino Suarez, the vice-president who was assassinated along with President Madero.

It was one of those beautiful mornings for which Mexico is famous when we moved into the outskirts of Mexico City—and into the sights and sounds of victory for the revolution. We shunted about for awhile in a railway yard amid crowds of jubilant soldiers. They were shouting back and forth and jesting, some singing La Cucaracha. Bands were playing. More troops were still arriving. Veterans of many campaigns were crowded inside and on top of boxcars, many accompanied by their womenfolk. On a plain beyond the tracks cavalry was massing as far as I could see. Soldiers, soldiers, soldiers. (To say that there were more soldiers here than I had ever seen before would have little meaning. I had never seen a larger military concentration than 700 Confederate veterans in a Memorial Day parade in Durham!) Historians have estimated the troops massed there at approximately 20,000.

Venustiano Carranza, Primer Jefe

Our train came to a stop at the station of Tlalnepantla. Carranza was already there. Flanked by aides and approached with great respect, he was emphatically the First Chief. General Obregon had already occupied Mexico City, but many arrangements had to be made before the formal entry of Carranza. Some of the group with whom I had come from Monterrey disappeared, but I continued to live on the train. The logistical situation at Tlalnepantla I no longer remember, but I know that I never wanted for a good meal. There was much coming and going, with colonels and generals most in evidence now.

Pushing through the crowd, I had several opportunities to watch Carranza. A tall, patriarchal figure with a long white beard, he had sometimes been called the Moses of the oppressed masses. But he was no hand-shaking man of the people. His bearing was of stiff dignity and monumental calm. He wore a big Stetson hat, an especially tailored field gray uniform, and dark glasses. Once, and once only, I spoke to the Great Man. Standing in a circle of American cameramen who were taking his picture, I heard someone say they ought to get him without his hat. I spoke out: "Abajo el sombrero, senor, por favor." And Carranza took off his hat.

Three young Americans from Texas joined our party at Tlalnepantla and I quickly made friends with them. They were like homefolks and it was a relief to be able to talk without having to struggle with Spanish. These fellows represented a banknote printing company. They were to have a vital role in the changeover in Mexico City, when a flood of new Constitucionalista currency would be needed. They rented an automobile and I joined them in several tours of the pretty countryside while we waited for the next move. I do not remember the exact details of that move except that there was a short train journey with a crowd of exciting people and many impressive uniforms. Cars were waiting at the Buena Vista station to take us to the Hotel Iturbide. That old hotel, once the palace of the Emperor Iturbide, had been taken over by the provisional government to house newly arrived officials. I was still a guest of the revolution.

The next day saw the triumphal entry of the First Chief. My Texas money-printing friends, who

Entrance of the Constitutionalist Army to Mexico City, August 1914.

seemed to be on the inside track to everything, invited me to go with them to view the spectacle from the National Palace. Two of them showed their passes at the big palace door and the four of us walked confidently in without being stopped. Climbing several flights of stairs to the roof, we found places over the balcony from which Carranza was expected to address the multitude. We looked down on the vast square called Zocalo, where a crowd was already beginning to gather. The victory parade was then moving down the Paseo de la Reforma. Soon a band began to play and a crack regiment of cavalry entered the square, followed by a long column of miscellaneous marching soldiers. At last Carranza appeared. He was riding a fine black horse, with General Obregon riding at his side. A group of other generals were close behind them. The parade went on and on—more soldiers and then civilian contingents, members of labor, agrarian and political organizations, carrying a variety of signs. The mainstream of the parade marched past the palace and moved on down a side street away from the plaza.

The Zocalo was now a sea of tightly-squeezed humanity. I was shocked to see mounted police using riding whips to make way through the crowd for the First Chief. A crowd of women, waiting outside the palace, pelted him with flowers, but both flowers and women were quickly lost in the crush of people. I saw several women faint. Carranza entered the palace and made his way to the balcony. When the last contingent of paraders had gone by, he made a speech. I do not remember what Carranza said—if I ever really knew—but there were many Vivas. The crowd at last dispersed, to go on celebrating in other places what many believed was the end of the long civil war.

More thoughtful observers were troubled over the absence from the celebration of Francisco Villa. For my part, I wished that I could have seen that exciting hero. I walked back to the Iturbide alone. Passing a sign which said "American Club," I went in to rest for a moment and see what the American Club was like. It was deserted except for one old man sitting by a window giving on to the street where the parade had gone by. He did not share the enthusiasm with which I was still tingling. He had seen Mexican governments overthrown before. "Before long," he said, "there'll be another big show like this. They'll be going crazy over Villa or somebody else."

My stay at the Hotel Iturbide as a guest of the provisional government and my friendly contact with the Mexican bureaucrats both came to a end in a few more days. I had a pleasant afternoon with Hector Bourges and I did some sightseeing alone. Incidentally, I called on Leon Canova, who was also installed at the Iturbide. Mr. Canova was one of those confidential agents whom President Wilson sent to Mexico during that period of turmoil. He chatted jovially with me for only a few minutes, avoiding any comment on Mexican politics. Then one morning I was called to the office of a senior official (I think it was Villareal), who informed me courteously that all the accommodations in the hotel would now be needed for still arriving government personnel. I moved out and took a room in the Hotel del Jardin. Apart from losing free lodging, I was sorry to leave the place where everybody I knew in Mexico was housed. The fact was that these men had already gone out of my life. Busy now with large affairs and having many people to see, they no longer seemed to recognize that American kid who had come down on the train with them from Monterrey.

Patio Hotel Iturbide, Mexico City.

My period of glory ended. I was no longer a companion of important people making history. I was just a lonely North Carolina boy in a great foreign city. For a week or more I went about by myself or with some friends of a day or two, all Americans, none of whose names I remember. I paid an overnight visit to Vera Cruz, which was still occupied by American troops. With fresh memories of the American attack, in which about 200 Mexicans lost their lives, there was a certain sullenness among the populace, but I ran into no personal unpleasantness.

Back in Mexico City a day or two later I met one Tomas Johnson, and that started another little chapter in my story. This man first drew me into conversation in a restaurant called El Vaso de Leche, where I was eating alone. I went back to El Vaso de Leche again and again, and Johnson and his wife more or less adopted me. Tomas Johnson was a big, hulking American-Mexican who had spent most of his 60 years south of the Rio Grand. His señora was a very unliberated little Mexican lady, who tended to mother me. My conversation with her had to be in Spanish, but I suppose I was ripe for a little mothering.

Johnson had a variety of mysterious interests which he talked to me about. He possessed a collection of herbs which, he said, had fantastic medicinal qualities, and he was in touch with Indians who were prepared to get him more in unlimited quantities. Once he had enough capital to exploit them, he was sure the herbs would make him a fortune. He also had a ranch and other extensive properties in the state of Sinaloa, but with the suspension of train service to that region due to the revolution he was cut off from those resources and was temporarily strapped. Still he was not entirely without cash and his credit was good at the small hotel adjoining El Vaso de Leche where the Johnsons lived—and into which I also moved. Mr. Johnson picked up the checks for my meals and had my room charged to his account. For my part I "lent" him my typewriter, on which he wrote many letters. I never knew who his correspondents were, but he evidently had many friends in influential quarters. (My typewriter was never returned or paid for.) He urged me to remain in Mexico and be a partner in his various enterprises. The señora begged me to stay.

Mr. Johnson fascinated me with stories of his experiences in Mexico during the turmoil of recent years. He knew all about revolutions. He had seen how they worked at the lower levels. It was easy to start one, but hard to accomplish anything with it. He had known a lot of revolutionists and they weren't worth a damn. The need was for some good men to get into the business. After a few hours of listening to this, I conceived a dream of becoming a Mexican myself and getting into a revolution. Whimsically at first and then more seriously on my part, we made some tentative plans. As soon as transportation returned to normal we would travel to his ranch, where I would be in charge of 20 or 30 ranch hands. After winning their loyalty, my influence would spread to the neighboring village and eventually through the state and beyond. When I remember this nonsense I am reminded of how young I was. Johnson's motivation in it all, I have never been able to fathom. At any rate my promise to my father to return home in the fall made all this talk a vain exercise for the time being. But the idea of embarking upon a career in Mexican politics stayed with me.

It was mid-September and time to start homeward, but that return to the United States presented a problem of the first magnitude. Railway passenger service to the north, except for military and government personnel, had not yet been resumed. I scanned the newspapers and made frantic inquiries, but there was no way for an ordinary person to buy a ticket and travel to Monterrey. (From Monterrey to the border at Laredo there was regular train service.) Finally an opportunity came to join an official party headed for Monterrey and I took my leave of the Johnsons with some emotion. The señora wept.

During the few days of my journey out of Mexico I found myself once more in an atmosphere of top brass and of history. How it was finagled I do not think I was fully aware at the time and there is another memory lapse at this point. I am sure only that Tomas Johnson had a hand in it. In his conspiratorial way he was a man of extraordinary capabilities. However that may have been, the next thing that I remember after saying goodbye to the Johnsons at their hotel is myself on board a train, and not just a train, but the presidential train. Its four old but still resplendent cars had been the official train of President Madero.

I also remember that I was already on terms of intimate friendship with a boy named Luis—who must have brought me to the train. Luis was just 16 years old, like me. He enjoyed practicing the English that he knew, but we talked in both languages. And we talked a great deal. His father was the reason at this point for the projected trip north. The latter's name was Pesquiera and I understood that he was the director general of railways in the new regime. During the several days that we waited in the train Señor Pesquiera came and went frequently and he had a number of visitors. Conferences were held in the drawing room car—which I entered only once, when Luis introduced me to his parents. Luis and I kept mainly to a sleeping compartment that he shared with me and the kitchen, when we were not loitering on the platform alongside the train. My closest friend next to Luis was the cook, an American blackman who said he had cooked for President Madero. He had spent many years in Mexico, but he still spoke English like a Negro from "down south". No one since I had left North Carolina reminded me so much of home as he.

Alas, I was not to travel on the presidential train. I believe this change had to do somehow with one General Cabral, although the name "Cabrera" also comes to mind. It seemed that the general had a sudden important mission somewhere in the north and my place on the train was needed for his aide. Luis was plainly disappointed when he broke the news to me, but he had arranged other transportation for me—and it was only a few degrees less glamorous.

Another train had been readied on a track nearby for General Antonio Villareal. The latter a brother, I think, of the Villareal whom I had met earlier. Besides being a powerful military leader he was governor of the state of Nuevo León. He was returning now to his capital, Monterrey. His train included Pullman accomodations for members of his staff and other associates. As a diplomatic courtesy a compartment had also been alloted to Señor Walls y Merino, the confidential agent of the King of Spain, who was returning to Spain via the United States. Through Luis' intervention, I was invited to share the compartment with that diplomat. Walls y Merino was a genial and considerate gentleman, who spoke beautiful English, and I enjoyed traveling with him. (He sent me a postcard later from Spain.)

My adventure in Mexico concluded with a last, momentary flash of pomp and circumstance, though my connection with it was accidental. General Villareal was returning from the wars and preparations had been made in Monterrey to receive him like a conquering hero. A crowd had gathered at the railway station, a band played and troops lined the street that the governor took. The taxicab of Walls y Merino and me, to our embarrassment was caught in the procession behind the governor's car until our driver found a way to escape down a side street to our hotel.

Troubles were mounting for Carranza when I left Mexico. The commanders of the revolution's two largest armies, Villa and Zapata, had held aloof from the First Chief in his hour of triumph. Villa was now openly hostile. Many others were dissatisfied with the stiff-necked Carranza, who seemed little inclined to push the land and social reforms for which they had fought. Villa was rising, Carranza declining. A convention was held in the city of Aguascalientes with the ostensible purpose of healing dissensions and forming a united movement. Nearly all the revolutionary factions, including the followers of Zapata, sent delegations to the convention, but Carranza would have nothing to do with it. Villa dominated the proceedings. A Villa henchman was appointed provisional president of the republic. The situation developed into a war between Carranza on the one hand and the convention and Villa on the other. On November 21, Carranza fled from Mexico City, and on December 2, Villa and Zapata went in. Carranza established his headquarters in Vera Cruz. He would come back in time and rule Mexico, but that was the situation which I observed from Trinity College as the year 1914 drew to a close.

I had returned home and had entered college only two weeks late. At first I talked volubly about my exciting summer and my rendezvous with history in Mexico, but I met with only bored or incredulous indifference on the part of my classmates. This was a keen disappointment and it annoyed me, though my resentment was mitigated by the reflection that, unlike me, those small-town youths were too ignorant to be interested in events on the world stage. I shut up about my adventures and became a recluse. The role of recluse suited me the more because of something that I was not prepared to mention to anyone—my dream of becoming a Mexican revolutionist. That dream stirred within me for about four more months, and then abruptly perished. My studies were badly neglected, except one subject, Spanish. On that I worked enthusiastically. The only teacher whom I came to know was the professor of Spanish literature, Dr. Albert Webb, a frisky, bearded little man whom the students referred to as "Rabbit" Webb. Professor Webb was tickled to find such an eager student as me. I called at his home evenings and he lent me an armful of Spanish novels, which I read one after another.

In my hours alone, I made plans for my future and the future of Mexico. I was living then with my family in Durham, though I conversed no more with them than I did with my classmates.

30

Except in bad weather when I took a street car, I walked the mile to the college each morning and walked back in the evening. I also did some walking on the campus and up a country road beyond. These walks were well suited to air castle building. Mexico was desperately in need of someone to lead it out of the mire of confusion and civil war and into an era of peace and progress. It might be that a young idealist like me, starting with a clean slate and no personal enmities, would be the kind of leader that Mexico needed. I realized that it would take time for me to rise to the top, or even

General Francisco "Pancho" Villa on horseback

to a position of influence, but there would be satisfactions along the way; and what more beautiful and romantic theater could be found than Mexico!

My name, "Ben Muse," had a foreign ring and would be an awkward household word in Mexico. I would call myself, I decided, Benito Musa. (Mexico's great national hero was Benito Juarez.) The area of planning to which I gave most thought was the problem of what kind of uniform my soldiers should wear. The big sombreros and the loose, baggy trousers that I had seen on so many of the soldiers at Tlalnepantla and in Mexico City would not do at all, although I realized that the uniform change would have to be gradual. Shorts like those worn by British soldiers in the tropics would be cheaper and more comfortable once Mexicans got used to them, although long trousers would be preferable in the cooler, mountainous areas. The big sombrero of course belonged to the very soul of Mexico and it should be worn by civilian country folk, but it should be banished as soon as practicable from the armed forces. Caps like those worn in the Mexican regular army and by revolutionary officers would be acceptable, but I hoped to design something better. I wanted to get a Roman touch somewhere, if only in the headgear; perhaps an inexpensive version of the Roman helmet could be contrived. The new uniforms would be white with red and green stripes down the sides, the colors of the Mexican flag. The dress uniform of elite regiments would require further study, but the Mexican eagle–and–serpent–on–the–cactus insignia was to be stamped on the tunics if possible.

Brass bands would be plentiful, they did so much for morale. My legions would march to stirring music. Discipline would be strict, but not cruelly enforced. The spirit of patriotism and martial glory that I would inspire would take care of that. There was no place in my dream for bloodshed. I do not recall that I envisioned any killing. I saw my soldiers always marching while bands played and people cheered. Of course, they would have to march to some purpose, and there would have to be something going on in offices. I planned in due course to study economic and social problems, but I was confident that the splendor of my regime would attract a pood of capital for industry and commerce and make possible all manner of reforms.

The reader may find this episode lacking in

credibility. Looking back 60 years later, I do not find it easy to understand. At 16 years of age, I should have known better. However, I tell it as it was—and I am not exactly ashamed.

I had abandoned now the technique that I had worked out with Tomas Johnson. I decided rather to align myself with one of the two contending factions in the present civil war. The choice was between Francisco Villa and Venustiano Carranza. Each of these, by the way, had a delegation in Washington lobbying for United States support. To me Villa was definitely more attractive than the old fuddy-duddy Carranza, who seemed to be on his way out anyway. To my great regret I had never seen Villa, but I had read about him and I had seen many pictures of him. He was quite the charismatic figure in the Mexican revolution. That famous photo of Pancho Villa galloping, like a lighthearted cowboy, at the head of a long column of rugged horsemen, was irresistible.

My infatuation with Villa requires some further explanation in the light of information in the many books and articles that have been written about him since. Something like an apology may be due to some of my present Mexican friends, who recall that sinverguenza with revulsion.

Pancho Villa was a pistol-happy murderer and libertine compared to whom the worst of the Bad Men of the Old West were like choir boys. But we had a different picture of him in the United States at the time. It must be said also that not a few decent and intelligent Mexicans put their faith in Francisco Villa. There were intellectuals around him and many very respectable officers in his army. I have in mind for instance General Felipe Angeles, a distinguished professional soldier and undeniably a gentleman. Villa had been a devoted follower of the lofty Madero. In the United States, before the disillusionment set in, he was widely regarded as a kind of Robin Hood. Some even called him a Sir Galahad! President Wilson had said that he was "a safe man to tie to," and Secretary of State William Jennings Bryan referred to him as an "idealist." With all this in mind, perhaps a 16-year-old boy in North Carolina would be forgiven for being pro-Villa in 1914.

Conclusion

In January 1915, I spent a few days with my uncle Alexander Potter in Washington. The ostensible purpose of my visit was to do some sight-seeing in the Nation's capital, but my secret purpose was something far more exciting. It was no less than to enlist in the army of Francisco Villa. I was able-bodied, and there were many youths of my age in the revolutionary armies. I was sure that, with my obvious qualities of mind and spirit, the Villa people would be glad to have me on their side.

No Mexican government being recognized at the time, the Carranza and Villa representatives in Washington did not have diplomatic status. They were called "confidential agents." The Villa confidential agency occupied one end of the fourth floor of the Powhatan Hotel (now the Roger Smith). It resembled one of the small legations with which I became acquainted later in the United States Foreign Service. The two secretaries to whom I introduced myself wore gray striped trousers and black foreign office coats like diplomats anywhere. They were suave and spoke correct English. I told them briefly the purpose of my visit. If they were astonished, they concealed the fact and listened politely. I asked to see the

Powhatan Hotel circa 1916

confidential agent himself, Senor Enrique C. Llorente. One secretary disappeared and returned in a few minutes to say that the confidential agent would receive me in about ten minutes.

While I waited, I sat in a comfortable anteroom before a large picture of General Villa. It was not like other pictures I had seen of Villa, but showed him looking dignified in a smart uniform. There were also pictures of Madero and Benito Juarez. I was surprised at the elegance of these surroundings and the elegance indeed of the two secretaries. All this seemed inappropriate somehow for the representatives of a man like Pancho Villa, but on reflection I conceived new respect for the dignity of the cause that I was about to espouse.

Enrique Llorente was a man whom I have always remembered with the greatest respect. One of Villa's intellectuals, he had long been a trusted adviser of that unlet-tered chieftain. A well-dressed middle-aged man of medium height, with slightly graying hair and a small mustache, he was not unlike an American official in appearance. Business was evidently slack in the agency, as he seemed to have plenty of time for me. I started talking in my laborious Spanish, but the conversation soon changed to English, which the confidential agent spoke fluently.

I told him about my great interest in Mexico and about my recent visit to his country. I was an admirer of General Villa and believed that he would lead the Mexican people at last to victory and peace. I wanted to become a Mexican citizen and spend my life working for the good of Mexico. I was anxious now to fight for liberty and justice in the army of General Villa.

Señor Llorente looked me over from head to foot several times while I was making this declaration. Then he was silent for a moment, but he did not laugh. He asked my age and inquired about Trinity College and my studies there. He asked if my father knew that I was coming to him with this proposal. My answer to that, of course, was No. Then he gave me some advice.

"Go back to your college," he said. "When you are older, if you still want to be a soldier, get into the United States Army. But I would advise you against even that—against joining any army. And, for God's sake, don't get into any revolution anywhere. You had better stay out of politics altogether. Stay out of politics. It is an uncertain affair and can cause you much grief in any country. Go into business or a profession." Concluding, he patted my shoulder as he shook my hand and said: "Go back to your college and study to be a good citizen of the United States."

I walked back from the Powhatan Hotel, several miles, to Uncle Alek's house east of the capital. I had come downtown on a street car, but I instinctively walked when I had something crucial to turn over in my mind.

www.ingramcontent.com/pod-product-compliance
Lightning Source LLC
Chambersburg PA
CBHW060507080526
44584CB00015B/1592